EXTINCT

EXTINCT
THYLACINE

Ben Garrod
Illustrated by Gabriel Ugueto

ZEPHYR

An imprint of Head of Zeus

This is a Zephyr book, first published in the UK in 2022
by Head of Zeus Ltd
This paperback edition first published in the UK in 2023
by Head of Zeus Ltd, part of Bloomsbury Publishing Plc

9 7 5 3 1 2 4 6 8

A catalogue record for this book is available from
the British Library.

ISBN (PB): 9781838935450
ISBN (E): 9781838935467

Typesetting and design by Nicky Borowiec

Printed and bound in Serbia by Publikum d.o.o.

Head of Zeus Ltd
5–8 Hardwick Street
London EC1R 4RG

WWW.HEADOFZEUS.COM

'The environment is our life'
Vanessa Nakate

CONTENTS

INTRODUCTION

For as long as there has been life on Earth, there has been extinction, and given enough time, all species will one day go extinct. Every day, it seems, we hear more and more tragic stories about more and more species being closer to extinction. There are scientists, conservationists, charities, universities, communities and even a few good governments fighting against extinction and trying to save some of our most treasured species and habitats. But, and there is a *but* to this story, extinction has its place in our world and, at the right level and at the right time, it is a perfectly natural occurrence and can even help evolution in some ways.

I am a scientist. It's the very best job in the world. In my work, I look at evolution and I've been lucky enough to spend time with some of the most endangered species on our planet, as well as a few that have already gone extinct. I'm fascinated by the effects extinction has on nature, in the broader sense. But how much do we *really* know about extinction?

If we are to ever stand a chance of saving species from extinction, then first we need to understand it. What is extinction? What causes it? What happens when many species go extinct at once? I want to explore extinction as a biological process and investigate why it can sometimes be a positive thing for evolution, as well as, at times, nature's most destructive force. Let's put it under the microscope and find out everything there is to know.

When a species goes extinct, we place a dagger symbol (†) next to its name when it's listed or mentioned in a scientific manner. So, if you do see the name of a species with a little dagger after it, you'll know why. It's extinct. In this series, I have written about eight fantastic species. Starting with *Hallucigenia* (†), then *Dunkleosteus* (†) and trilobites (†), through to *Lisowicia* (†), *Tyrannosaurus rex* (†) and megalodon (†), before finishing with thylacine (†)

and lastly, the Hainan gibbon. Of these, only the Hainan gibbon does not have a dagger next to its scientific name, meaning it is the only animal we still have a chance of saving from extinction.

Professor Ben Garrod

WHAT IS EXTINCTION?

EXTINCTION IS the death of a species. Individual animals, and other organisms, die all the time. It's sad, of course, especially when we know and care about that individual, whether it's a loved pet, or a well-known zoo inhabitant, or even a famous individual from the wild. Losing a group of individuals can be really tough. There are lots of examples where populations of seabirds have been wiped out by a storm, communities of whales lost to toxic chemicals, or fields of rare flowers illegally dug up by collectors.

As sad as the loss of an individual or population of individuals is, in the bigger picture, the overall survival of that species is safe. But extinction is different. When a species is extinct, there is no second chance, there are no other populations safely in reserve, there will be no more of its kind. Despite glimmers of hope offered from some very cool areas of science, such as creating clones or altering

DNA to resurrect lost species, extinction is the full stop on the last line on the final page in the story of the life of that species on Earth.

Extinction affects habitats, it alters ecosystems, it changes ecologies. Nature is a finely connected web of millions of different species from groups that make up the entire web of life, and the gentlest tug on one strand can affect the whole thing. Extinctions can be like this and even the loss of a small and seemingly insignificant species can have major and long-lasting impacts across the planet. If you don't believe me, ask a scientist what would happen if we were to lose bees.

Extinction has been present since the first life on Earth popped into existence, which must mean that loads *and loads* of species have gone extinct. It's hard to get your head around how many. Scientists predict that as many as 99 per cent of the species that have *ever* lived have gone extinct, and if you're wondering how many species that might be, then if their calculations are correct, it means we have already lost an almost unbelievable five billion species from our planet.

We can't be certain though, because many extinctions stretch back millions (or even hundreds of millions) of years, and as there wasn't a scientist there with a camera or a notebook, we shall never know about many of these losses. Scientists believe that there may be 10–14 million different species (although some believe this figure might even be as high as one trillion). Of those, only 1.2 million have been documented and recorded in a proper scientific way, meaning we don't know about 90 per cent of life on planet Earth right now.

Here's where it gets a little complicated. Extinction is natural. Even we human beings will go extinct one day. We are simply one of those 14 million or so species, remember. Usually, a species has about 10 million years or so of evolving, eating, chasing, playing, maybe doing homework, building nests or even going to the moon before it goes extinct and ends up in the history (or even *prehistory*) books. Some species last longer than this, some are around for less time.

Extinction is a wholly natural process and, in many ways, helps create the rich and dazzling diversity we see across the natural world, but it has a time and place. Just because something happens naturally sometimes, it doesn't mean it's always OK to stand back and let it happen. If we understand the processes behind extinction, we have a better chance not only of knowing when to step in or not, but importantly, it might also just help us avoid getting caught up in a catastrophic mass extinction ourselves.

WHY DO SPECIES GO EXTINCT?

HAVE YOU ever really thought about the phrase 'what goes up, must go down' and what it means? It's about consequences and the natural cycles of things. It's the same idea as 'all good things must come to an end', and we can think of species in this way too. They evolve and live their own story for a while, whether that's photosynthesising the sun's light into energy, swimming across oceans or swinging through the trees. Then their story inevitably ends as they slip (or are pushed) into extinction. The differences between these evolutionary stories are the really interesting bits, though, as well as differences in how long a species exists. There are different reasons for that species' story coming to an end. Sometimes, these are obvious, such as hunting being responsible for the loss of the passenger pigeons in the early 20th century. The causes behind the loss of other species can be less clear and more confusing, and sometimes, the loss of another species can be a combination of causes.

There are almost limitless reasons which might lead to extinction, but they have one thing in common. They all focus on a change. These changes can be either in the physical environment of the species, such as the actual destruction of a habitat, flooding or drought. The change might be in its 'biological environment', such as the arrival of a new predator or the development of a new deadly disease. If the species does not have enough time to change or simply cannot change, then it will die out and become extinct. There are a variety of general causes that can lead, directly or indirectly, to the extinction of a species or group of species.

DISEASES, PREDATION AND COMPETITION

Diseases are often linked to extinction. Practically every species alive has its own set of diseases and those which it can pick up from other species. In 2006, in a cave near New York, a bat was found with a weird white fungus around its nose. This random discovery turned out to be the first time that a terrible disease called white-nose syndrome was seen in bats in North America. Within a few years, an estimated six million bats had died, with numbers of some species dropping by as much as 99 per cent.

Think of a predator and I can almost guarantee you're picturing either a shark, polar bear, eagle or one of the big cats. I bet you didn't think of an invertebrate and I can guarantee you didn't think of a snail.

O'ahu tree snail

But predators come in all shapes and sizes and any of them can cause the extinction of other species, given the right (or wrong) situation. Usually, predators and prey live in some sort of balance. They have both evolved to live side by side for hundreds of thousands, if not millions, of years. This is what we call coevolution, where the evolution of two species is closely tied together. But when a predator is suddenly introduced into an environment, the prey has no time to evolve to avoid being eaten. Once a predator is introduced into a new environment, there is often little that can be done to prevent the consequences.

There are a few species of snails found on Hawaii that are found nowhere else on Earth. In the mid-1930s, giant African

Rosy wolfsnail

land snails were introduced to the island, apparently because they'd look nice in gardens and because they could be eaten. Their population then boomed, so to try to control their numbers, a *different* species of snail, the rosy wolfsnail, was introduced. The rosy wolfsnail was supposed to eat the introduced African land snail, but instead, it went after other prey. It preferred O'ahu tree snails, which were native to Hawaii. Within a few years, several species of tree snails had been hunted to extinction, because of the introduced predator, which some call the 'cannibal snail'.

Giant African
land snail

Nature works in balance, where each environment evolves to have the right combination of herbivores, carnivores and omnivores, predators and prey and different types of plants, fungi and other organisms. Some of those species compete with one another but there are usually some differences in behaviour or anatomy between them, which helps them avoid too many problems with each other.

But when a species, or group of species, is introduced into the habitat of another species, or another group, then the competition hasn't had time to balance out and instead, it can lead to biological catastrophe. Some of these problems between competitors can be because humans have introduced a species, or because new species naturally evolve, or because competitors naturally find their way into new environments.

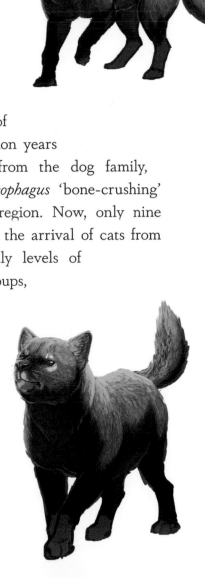

The group containing dogs, wolves, foxes and their relatives evolved in North America after the fall of the dinosaurs. Around 22 million years ago, more than 30 species from the dog family, including the now-extinct *Borophagus* 'bone-crushing' dogs, were found across the region. Now, only nine species remain. It appears that the arrival of cats from Africa and Asia caused deadly levels of competition between the two groups, leading to the extinction of as many as 30 species from the dog group.

Borophagus

Before species of cats arrived in North and South America, lots of species of dogs and their relatives were there. Borophagine (bor-O FAY-JEEN) or 'bone-crushing' dogs are hunting a six-horned pronghorn *Hexameryx* (hex-a mer-iks) in Florida, about five million years ago.

The end of the moa.

COEXTINCTION

Sometimes, a species has evolved alongside another species so closely that when one goes extinct, there is nothing the other can do but go extinct too. This might be a specific parasite depending on a specific host species or maybe a particular pollinating insect needing one species of plant in order to survive. An extreme example of a coextinction is the moa and the Haast's eagle. Moa were huge flightless birds found on New Zealand, with some being as much as 3.6m in height and 230kg in weight. The Haast's eagle was their main predator. When human settlers hunted the last moa into extinction around 600 years ago, the eagles were left with no food and they too went extinct.

GENETIC MIXING

Every organism has its own set of genetic data unique to that particular species. When you look past the physical parts and behaviours which help define a species, you get down to the genetic blueprint, and any small tweaks can change one species into another.

Japanese giant salamanders are the second-largest salamander species in the world and reach a length of up to 1.5m, weighing as much as 23kg. Like other salamanders, they primarily 'breathe' through their skin, they have amazing regenerative capabilities and are able to regrow skin and even bone. Only the Chinese giant salamanders are bigger, and it's this larger species that is helping drive the Japanese giant salamanders into extinction.

Chinese giant salamanders were introduced to several locations across Japan, where they bred with the salamanders already there. Now, in some habitats, especially around the city of Kyoto, there is a risk that the salamanders will be a mix of the two species. Over time, it's possible that the population of Japanese giant salamanders will drop and drop towards extinction and they'll be replaced by a 'new' hybrid species made up from the two.

Offspring are produced as a result of mixing the genetic material from both parents, so what's the problem? It's true that you, me and much of the animal kingdom result from this sort of genetic combo, but (I assume) your parents are the *same* species as one another. I'm pretty sure mine are. The problems only pop up when different species produce offspring, as this can lead to genetic problems or even unwanted physical effects.

HABITAT DESTRUCTION

When we talk about this cause of extinction, we usually use the phrase 'habitat loss' but we don't lose habitats, we destroy them. Admitting this is a step in the right direction needed to protect many habitats and ecosystems around the world. The saddest thing about habitat destruction is that it means devastation not only for individual organisms but also sometimes for entire species. Habitat destruction has always featured significantly as a cause of extinctions throughout the history of life on Earth.

Even within the ecosystem in which the subject of this book, thylacines, evolved, habitat was lost and this would have affected the species. When habitat change or destruction is an influence for extinction, it might be because that habitat is completely removed, or maybe poisoned, or its temperature has changed. A whole host of changes to a habitat can bring about an extinction event.

CLIMATE CHANGE

There's a reason winters are becoming milder, summers wetter, fiercer hurricanes more frequent, huge bush fires ravage continents, massive floods regularly damage landscapes, frequent droughts cause famines and coral reefs are destroyed. The chemistry of oceans is changing dangerously and polar ice is melting at a scary rate.

All these, and many more issues, are as a result of climate change. We used to call it global warming, but we now know it's more complicated and that climate change is a complex problem with a whole series of effects.

One place that *is* getting warmer, however, is the Arctic. It's a vast area which is showing massive amounts of change right now. Even as I'm sitting here writing I was shocked to read that while much of Europe is much colder than you'd expect for early summer, one of the warmest places anywhere in Europe today is in the Arctic, which reached an unbelievable 30.5°C. By reaching such high temperatures, changes in the Arctic will affect the climate, weather and environments across the planet. Climate change puts trillions and trillions of animals, plants and other organisms at risk, meaning millions of species face being pushed into extinction.

All over the planet, habitats, environments and ecosystems are being damaged, destroyed and lost because of climate change. Huge glaciers and ice sheets in Antarctica are melting at a scary rate.

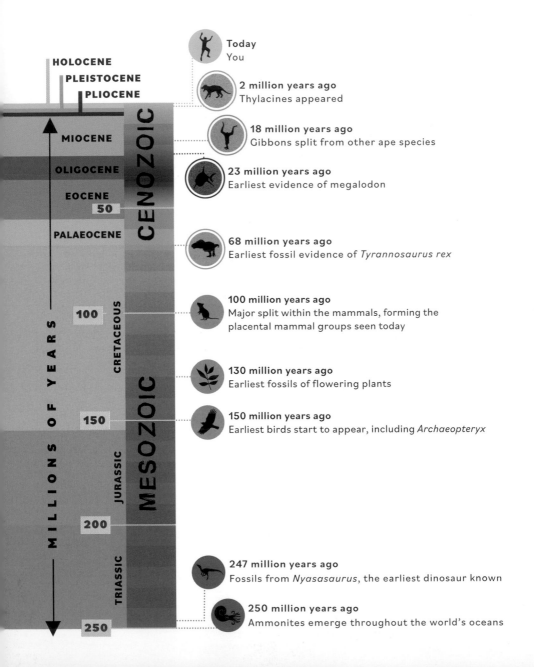

HOLOCENE
PLEISTOCENE
PLIOCENE

MIOCENE

OLIGOCENE

EOCENE
50

PALAEOCENE

CENOZOIC

100

CRETACEOUS

MESOZOIC

150

JURASSIC

200

TRIASSIC

250

MILLIONS OF YEARS

Today
You

2 million years ago
Thylacines appeared

18 million years ago
Gibbons split from other ape species

23 million years ago
Earliest evidence of megalodon

68 million years ago
Earliest fossil evidence of *Tyrannosaurus rex*

100 million years ago
Major split within the mammals, forming the placental mammal groups seen today

130 million years ago
Earliest fossils of flowering plants

150 million years ago
Earliest birds start to appear, including *Archaeopteryx*

247 million years ago
Fossils from *Nyasasaurus*, the earliest dinosaur known

250 million years ago
Ammonites emerge throughout the world's oceans

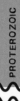

MILLIONS OF YEARS

PALAEOZOIC

PERMIAN

300

CARBONIFEROUS

350

DEVONIAN

400

SILURIAN

450

ORDOVICIAN

500

CAMBRIAN

PROTEROZOIC

ARCHEAN

300 million years ago
Lisowicia first appeared

320 million years ago
'Mammal-like reptiles', including *Dimetrodon*, evolve

340 million years ago
Earliest amphibians

382 million years ago
Earliest evidence of *Dunkleosteus*

385 million years ago
Oldest fossilised tree

400 million years ago
Earliest fossils of insects

Some of the dates for earliest fossils are estimates based on our best understanding right now. They are not always perfect and the more evidence we collect, the more certain we can be and the more accurate these dates will eventually become.

500 million years ago
Fossil evidence from *Hallucigenia*

520 million years ago
Earliest vertebrates emerged (and may have looked like small eels)

530 million years ago
Earliest fossils of trilobites

680 million years ago
Earliest ancestors of jellyfish and their relatives

2.15 billion years ago
Earliest evidence of bacteria

3 billion years ago
Earliest evidence of viruses

MASS
EXTINCTIONS

RIGHT NOW, somewhere in the world, something, for some reason, will be going extinct, hopefully due to natural causes. In the same way that the evolution and appearance of a species is completely natural, so too is the constant loss of species. Species come and go in a cycle, a bit like tides moving back and forth or the changing of the seasons.

Extinction is unavoidable and goes on at a fairly predictable rate wherever life exists. We call this background extinction: constant, low-level extinction which doesn't cause major problems on a wider scale, other

Mammoth

than for the species going extinct. These 'every day extinctions' go mostly unnoticed by the majority of us. This all changes when we talk about a mass extinction.

For the purposes of my books, we are going to treat a mass extinction as the worldwide loss of around 75 per cent (or more) of species, over a short space of 'geological' time. If you're wondering how short 'a short space of geological time' is, then let's say it has to be under three million years. This might sound like a very long time, but remember Earth is around four and a half *billion* years old. By making our timeframe three million years we can

Labrador duck

Pterosaur

catch the sudden and disastrous mass extinctions, such as the dinosaur-killing asteroid End Cretaceous event, as well as some of the mass extinctions which played out over hundreds of thousands or even millions of years ago.

Throughout the series, as well as focusing on the five 'classic' mass extinctions, we'll look at the newly discovered mass extinction which claimed the mighty megalodon. We'll also look at the current extinction event which is being triggered by us, and at what scientists and conservationists are doing to tackle that threat.

Megaloceros

THE ANTHROPOCENE MASS EXTINCTION

THE LIST of mass extinction events isn't long but each changed the face of our planet, and each was unique, either in the way it was caused or in the effects it had. One was started by a hurtling asteroid, one by an unimaginably large lava field, another, we think, was even caused by plants. No mass extinction, however, has been caused by a single species. Until now. There's some discussion about whether we're entering a mass extinction, or whether

we're already in one. Is this the sixth mass extinction, the seventh, eighth, etc? What we can't argue with is that regardless of what number mass extinction this and how far into it we might be, one species is to blame. That's our species. Humans.

Because humans are causing such an impact on Earth's environments and the species which inhabit them, we've adopted a new name for this time period and this particular mass extinction. It's called the Anthropocene (an-throp O-SEEN) period and the Anthropocene mass extinction. The name Anthropocene comes from the Ancient Greek 'anthropos', meaning 'human', and 'cene', which means 'recent' or 'new'. The Anthropocene falls within the timeframe called the Holocene (hol-O SEEN), which started just over 11,500 years ago.

Scientists haven't yet completely accepted the Anthropocene, so there's still discussion over exactly when it started. Some believe it should be recorded as having

started between 15,000 and 12,000 years ago, when we see human agriculture start. With the development of farming, habitats changed, animals which competed with farming were hunted, and livestock replaced wild animals in many places. Others believe the Anthropocene started around the year 1500, when we see an increase in the rates of extinctions in the historical records of species around the world, showing a higher count than would be expected with the normal level of everyday, 'background' extinctions. Others think that the point when the first atomic bomb was dropped in 1945, ending the Second World War, should mark the start of the Anthropocene. As discussions between scientists continue, we should have a better definition of the Anthropocene in the next few years.

The Anthropocene is the only mass extinction where we know exactly how different species, such as the thylacine (thy-la-SEEN), were affected and were, or are, being driven into the history books.

The thylacine lived alongside a range of different plants, fungi and other animals, such as giant, bulbous-nosed wombats. Thylacines were an essential part of their ecosystem.

CAUSES

When we look at the mass extinctions which act as impactful chapters in the story of life on Earth, it's hard to untie exactly what happened to particular species within the mass extinction. We don't know, for example, what specifically happened to the last *Hallucigenia* at the end of the Ordovician period, or where the last megalodon hunted her prey, or on which day the last remaining *Tyrannosaurus rex* finally closed its eyes. But the Anthropocene mass extinction is different. We have a detailed, blow-by-blow account of what led some species into extinction and, sadly, what is leading to the extinction of more than one million other species right now.

Among these, the detailed extinction of the thylacine is an example which reads like a very sad story and one which should serve as a warning to us all. The thylacine lived all over Australia until around 4,000 years ago, when they disappeared from the mainland, most likely as a result from competition with dingoes, which had recently been introduced there. Remaining on Tasmania, the thylacine survived into the 20th century, before the last known one died in 1936 in Hobart zoo.

In the hundred years or so before the last thylacine died, European settlers and the local government had worked hard to trap, persecute and kill thylacines, in a plan to intentionally eradicate them from the environment. Farming was, and is, important in Tasmania and, quite rightly, people want to defend and protect their livelihoods. If a wild predator that looks like a cross between a wolf and a tiger is hunting your sheep every night, then it's understandable that you'd want them gone, especially if they were blood-thirsty, aggressive and dangerous killers. But it appears that this was a case of biological fake news. Thylacines were unlikely to be able to kill animals as large as an adult sheep, so were equally unlikely to be responsible for the killings. Dogs and human sheep thieves were most likely the guilty parties, as well as poor management of farm animals in some places. But as you can imagine, most people were happier blaming something that looked like the big, bad (stripy) wolf.

People actually received a reward for every thylacine they shot, trapped and poisoned, around £1 for every adult thylacine. As many as 3,500 were killed, with the last wild one shot dead in 1930. After this, only a few were left in zoos around the world. Still the hunting continued. It was only in 1936, 59 days before the last known animal, Benjamin, died in a zoo, that the Tasmanian government passed legal protection to stop the extinction of the thylacine. Although this was a positive step, it came way too late, as the thylacine was already most likely extinct in the wild.

Since Benjamin's death, many people, groups and expeditions have been out looking for signs that thylacines might still be alive in Tasmania. Even now, there are semi-regular reports of stripy, dog-like animals seen walking in remote parts of the island. Without any firm evidence that the thylacine is still around, the species was finally, and officially, declared extinct 50 years later, in 1986.

However, more than 1,200 records of sightings and pieces of physical evidence were collected by scientists at the University of Tasmania between 1910 and 2019. They looked at each of these reports and put the results together to see what the likelihood was that there might still be thylacines alive in the wild. Their study suggests the thylacine may have survived, in very small numbers, up until around the year 2000. Other studies disagree and have stated that the chances of the thylacine being around are about 1 in 1.6 trillion, and that there's a small chance they survived past the 1940s. At the other end of the scale, some believe there's as much as a one-in-ten chance of these beautiful predators remaining in the wild today. If you want to know what I think... well, what I *really* want to believe and what I actually believe based on the evidence are two very different things. I would dearly love to be proved wrong though.

The thylacine is just one victim of this most recent mass extinction. It was hunted into extinction. This might make the thylacine unique in terms of extinct animals, as it may be the only one to be intentionally driven extinct. The first part of the Anthropocene mass extinction is historical: species such as the dodo went extinct somewhere between 1662 and 1692, the Steller's sea cow disappeared in 1768, the great auk was lost in 1844, and elephant birds may have survived until as recently as 1880. Many of these were unintentionally and carelessly hunted into extinction, but more recently, as the Anthropocene mass extinction intensified, the causes increased in their numbers and their impact on every species of organism across the planet.

Once people were offered money to poison, trap and shoot thylacines, it wasn't long before they were close to extinction.

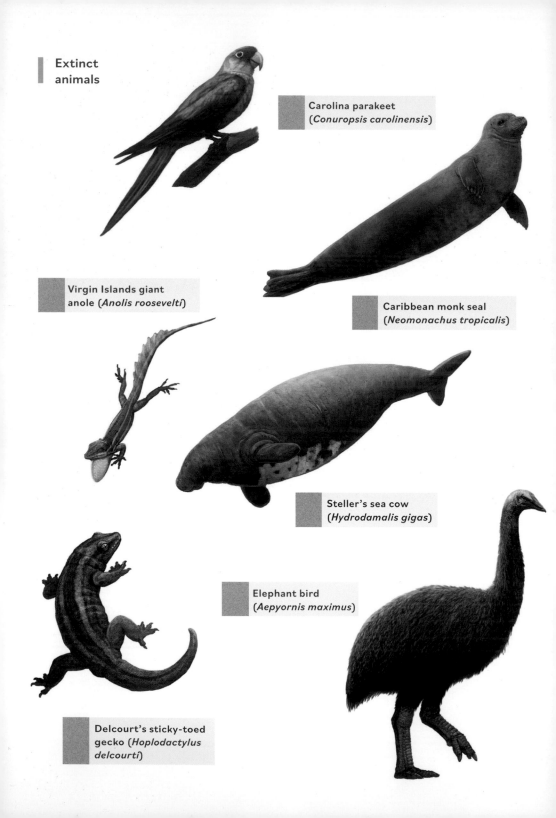

Extinct animals

Carolina parakeet
(*Conuropsis carolinensis*)

Virgin Islands giant
anole (*Anolis roosevelti*)

Caribbean monk seal
(*Neomonachus tropicalis*)

Steller's sea cow
(*Hydrodamalis gigas*)

Elephant bird
(*Aepyornis maximus*)

Delcourt's sticky-toed
gecko (*Hoplodactylus
delcourti*)

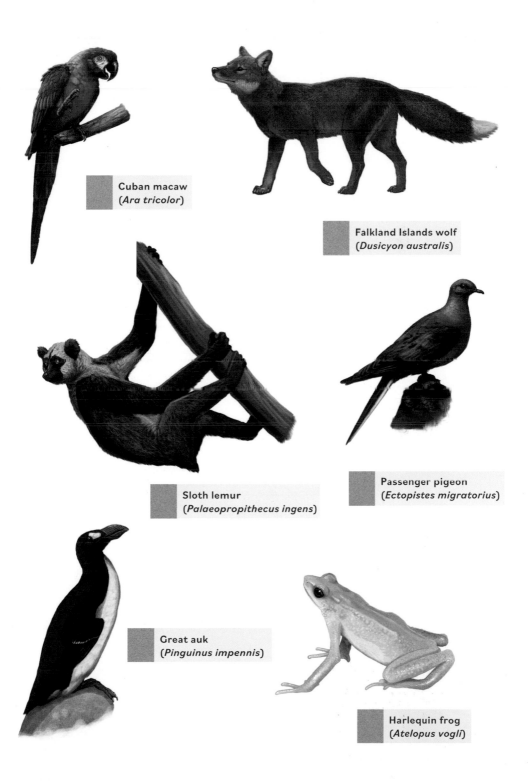

Cuban macaw
(*Ara tricolor*)

Falkland Islands wolf
(*Dusicyon australis*)

Sloth lemur
(*Palaeopropithecus ingens*)

Passenger pigeon
(*Ectopistes migratorius*)

Great auk
(*Pinguinus impennis*)

Harlequin frog
(*Atelopus vogli*)

EFFECTS

As we are living through the early stages of a mass extinction, it's already pretty clear, and shocking, that the effects can be seen all around us. Habitats and entire environments are being destroyed, local and global climate conditions are being affected, and biodiversity across the planet is being wiped out at an incredible rate.

The early stages of the Anthropocene mass extinction were dominated by hunting and exploitation. Some species, such as the dodo, were also influenced by the introduction of alien species. Now, I don't mean little green dudes with stun guns who arrive from outer space in silvery flying saucers. To a biologist, the term 'alien species' means any species that has been accidentally or intentionally introduced into an ecosystem which has formed without them being a part of it. Goats, dogs, cats, pigs, black rats, brown rats, some mongooses, lionfish, brown tree snakes and a whole list of others are all alien species. The problem is that many

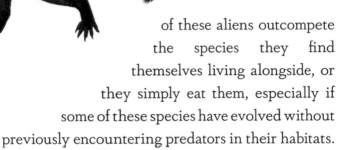

of these aliens outcompete the species they find themselves living alongside, or they simply eat them, especially if some of these species have evolved without previously encountering predators in their habitats.

These early stages of the mass extinction appear to have been selective and either targeted predators, such as the thylacine, animals which could be eaten, such as the Steller's sea cow, or those like the dodo that lived on islands and were vulnerable to hunting, alien species and habitat changes.

When we strip away the emotional attachments we have towards our own species and try to look at what we are and the impact we have on other species, it quickly becomes clear that we are in a category of our own.

We are a 'global superpredator', as we disrupt food chains around the world and have a record of hunting and killing the top predators across different ecosystems. Only a superpredator is able to do that. *Tyrannosaurus rex* did it, as did *Dunkleosteus*, but their reach was limited. Ours, however, is not and our actions have affected many groups of fungi, plants and animals, including mammals, birds, amphibians, reptiles, fish and invertebrates, throughout Africa, Asia, Europe, Australia, North America, South America and many small oceanic islands.

When we think of the asteroid at the end of the Cretaceous period, 66 million years ago, which killed off most of the dinosaurs, it's way too easy to think the asteroid struck and destroyed everything. If you watch cartoons and action films, that's certainly what it looked like, but actually, a load of different things contributed to this mass extinction. The asteroid created tsunamis and earthquakes, it released huge amounts of deadly gases, created millions of tonnes of ash which increased the temperature of the planet and prevented photosynthesis.

Suddenly, this single event becomes complicated – the more factors there were, the greater the impact. The asteroid killed many animals but the other factors combined to destroy ecosystems and push entire groups into extinction.

And now, we are experiencing the same with the Anthropocene mass extinction. Humans are responsible and in the early stages, most of the damage has been limited to individual species and specific habitats. But like the asteroid, things have become a *lot* worse as the different influences combine.

The Anthropocene mass extinction continues into the 21st century and the rate of extinction of species is somewhere between 100 and 1,000 times higher than you'd expect if extinctions were at a normal level. With land clearance and resources being used up by our demand for farm animals for their meat, overfishing in marine environments, increasing acidic conditions in our oceans, pollution, hunting, habitat destruction, alien species, introduced diseases and climate change, life on our planet is facing its greatest threat in at least 66 million years.

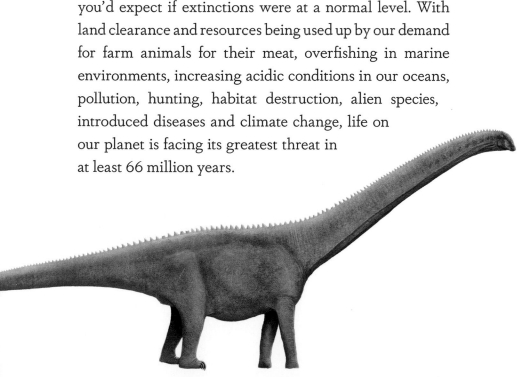

We might notice the loss of big or iconic species, such as whales or elephants or the thylacine, but it's the loss of some of the smallest species that will have the most dramatic effects. In a piece of research, scientists have found that numbers of microscopic plants within the oceans, or marine phytoplankton (FI-tow plank-tun), have massively dropped since the middle of the 20th century, and that within the last 60 or 70 years, warming within the oceans caused by climate change has led to a drop of around 40 per cent of the phytoplankton within our oceans. In the last few years especially, the rate of this loss has been increasing more rapidly.

These microscopic plants feed fish, which feed other marine species. If the levels of these marine plants drop, then it could lead to the extinction of seabirds, seals, whales, sharks and other fish and could mean *you* can't eat fish and chips as easily. Fewer plants in the oceans means less carbon dioxide can be absorbed from the atmosphere, which in turn will increase the warming of the atmosphere. This is just one example showing how environments are being affected by our actions.

As many as 7 per cent of all species on Earth may have been lost to extinction during the start of the Anthropocene mass extinction. Although we have a long way to go before we see the loss of the 75 per cent that identifies a true mass extinction, this already translates as millions of species, big and small. A worrying estimate is that since our own species started building cities and developed serious farming practices, as many as 83 per cent of wild mammals have disappeared.

Now, if we put all the mammals on the planet in a massive pile, we'd see that farm animals represent around 60 per cent of that pile. Humans would be approximately 36 per cent, and wild mammals a tiny 4 per cent. With as many as 25 per cent of plant and animal species currently threatened with extinction, we should all be looking at what we can do to stop this number growing and at what needs to be done to protect species currently under threat. The thylacine is just one among millions of species to be affected by the Anthropocene mass extinction.

This female orangutan has lost her forest home, which was illegally burned down so large companies could grow oil palm. Right now, at least one million species are threatened with extinction. The destruction of habitats and ecosystems increases the speed and severity of extinctions.

Professor Amy Dickman is a Professor at the University of Oxford, and is the Director of the Wildlife Conservation Research Unit (WildCRU). She also runs an African conservation project called Lion Landscapes. She studies wildlife, particularly large carnivores, with a focus on better understanding what we can do to help humans and dangerous species live alongside one another more successfully.

Why are predators important in conservation?

Predators (animals that kill and eat other animals) are often seen as scary and vicious. Think of the wolves in many childhood storybooks and of species such as vultures which are unfairly seen as ugly and unclean. Spotted hyenas get some of the worst press: despite being powerful hunters and having an interesting biology due to their scavenging tendencies, they have long been associated with death, witchcraft and evil spirits. In Japan, bears are deeply feared and thought to cause 'spiritual damage' if people so much as see them. Sharks are top predators and frequently demonised. Shark attacks on humans get huge media attention, even though people actually kill far more sharks than the other way around.

But human fascination with these species goes both ways. Much as we fear them – and often for good reason – we also love dangerous predators. Our interest in them has existed for

millennia, as shown by the extensive cave art of lions in France, painted more than 30,000 years ago. Throughout the ages, predatory animals have been used as symbols of courage, royalty, wisdom and power, and have adorned everything from coats of arms to sports team logos today. Despite – or perhaps even because of – the dangers they can pose, we are often drawn to predators, especially the largest and most untamed among them.

This means that predators can become powerful symbols for conservation. People are more engaged by predators than by other animals, and more likely to respond to campaigns and read articles that feature them. Top predators are major attractions for tourists, who will pay large sums of money to visit areas where those species live. This is useful because large predators such as lions, tigers and wolves need lots of prey to survive, meaning that large, intact habitats have to be conserved for them. The revenue from tourism, therefore, is important.

In those habitats, predators play vital ecological roles. Sick or weak prey are most likely to be hunted and killed, which keeps wildlife populations healthier and in check. Scavenging predators break down carcasses - a spotted hyena's massive jaw can crack open a giraffe's thigh bone - and return nutrients to the ecosystem. The presence of top predators indicates thriving ecosystems, so focusing on predator conservation helps secure lesser acknowledged, but equally important, biodiversity.

Conservation of predators is not simple. These animals often rely on human-dominated land that is beyond any protected areas reserved for them. They can kill people and their livestock, and are often killed in retaliation. This conflict is common and has terrible consequences for both people and wildlife. There is plenty that can be done: conservationists are working hard to better protect people and predators from one another, and to ensure that the presence of predators generates benefits for people, from a local to national level. This work will help enable our coexistence in the future, and safeguard these fascinating and important species for many more years to come.

THYLACINE

WE OFTEN GET ideas in our heads and jump to conclusions based on assumptions that aren't always right. One animal about which there are a *load* of assumptions is the thylacine, or Tasmanian tiger, which was found across Papua New Guinea, the Australian mainland and Tasmania. First, when we hear the term 'extinct' it's easy to think of some poor animal that disappeared millions of years ago. When you hear that an animal is stripy and has 'tiger' in its common name, then only one animal pops into your mind. If you've heard the word 'marsupial', you might think the group is all about kangaroos and wallabies.

And if you were told that a predator was hunted into extinction because of the threat it posed to sheep and other farm animals, then you might even wonder whether that predator might have had it coming. So, tempting as it might be to think of the thylacine as a dangerous, tiger-like predator that died out millions of years ago, nothing could be further from the truth. And, as the thylacine

A mother and her joeys watch their neighbours. Thylacines had a reputation as dangerous predators that threatened people, dogs and sheep. None of this was true. They were intelligent, beautiful and social animals.

shows, there's a *lot* more to the marsupial group than just kangaroos and wallabies.

There are so many examples of plants, animals and other organisms that have gone extinct, but few are sadder than the loss of the thylacine. The loss of this beautiful, iconic and unique predator should also make us angry, because although every species will go extinct at some point, *when* and *how* a species goes extinct varies massively. And sometimes, some of those extinctions are at completely the wrong time and for completely the wrong reasons. The thylacine might just be at the top of that list.

There are a number of reasons this iconic little predator went extinct, first in Australia and then Tasmania. After the last wild thylacine had been shot dead in 1930, Benjamin was the last of his species. He had been taken from the wild and put in a zoo, where he eventually died after being accidentally locked outside one exceptionally cold night. He was unable to survive the freezing conditions and when the keepers turned up on the morning of 7 September 1936, they found the last known thylacine dead. And with the loss of Benjamin, the species was extinct.

DISCOVERY

As scientists, we have to be careful when we say we have discovered something, because sometimes we have done no such thing. There are often stories about scientists discovering a 'brand-new species' in a rural part of Africa or a remote region in Asia, where in fact, local communities have known about the species for years. When we say that a new species has been discovered, do we mean it's been discovered by scientists, or westerners, or is it the first time it's ever been seen by any human ever? Unless it's the last of these, we cannot claim we've discovered a species or made a scientific breakthrough. It would be rude, disrespectful and in some situations even racist not to give credit where it's due.

When we look at the thylacine, we can say it was discovered in 1824, because that's when it was given its name. Or we could say it was discovered in 1808, because that's when it was first scientifically described, by someone with the fancy title of Tasmania's Deputy Surveyor-General. Maybe we can say the thylacine was actually discovered earlier, back in 1792, on

13 May, to be precise. This was when European (French) explorers first encountered the animal and a naturalist wrote about it in his diary.

If we want to go back to when the thylacine was first *discovered* and even when they were first described, we have to go back long before Europeans settled in Australia and well over a thousand years before the first scientist was anywhere near the region. It seems that the thylacine was first identified by the aboriginal people of Australia, as ancient rock art painted on cave walls or on the faces of protected rocky overhangs, and which has survived until today, shows us. Some of these beautiful thylacine images, often made using red pigment, are over a thousand years old, and may even be much older, possibly dating back as much as tens of thousands of years.

ANATOMY

One of my favourite phrases is 'never judge a book by its cover'. We say this because it's always worth remembering that while it might be easy to assume something based on looks, you never know what the real story is, and you might be in for a surprise. The thylacine is definitely a good example to highlight why you should not judge something based on appearance. The name 'thylacine' roughly translates as 'dog-headed pouched one'. It also has common names including the Tasmanian tiger and marsupial wolf, but although it loosely shared some characteristics with both tigers and wolves, its anatomy was very different to both.

Despite me saying the thylacine was different to both tigers and wolves, it did look a *little* bit like a cross between a tiger and a wolf. It was sandy yellow-brown to grey in colour and had between 15 and 20 distinct dark stripes across its back, running from its shoulders down to its tail, helping give it the name tiger. These stripes were darker in younger thylacine, but appeared to fade as they grew older.

The head was large and dog-like or wolf-like, which led to its other common name, the marsupial wolf. It had 46 teeth and although it had some well-developed muscles around its jaws, the jaws did not appear to be strong enough to kill sheep, as was so often reported.

One feature for which the thylacine was famous was the ability to open its jaws ridiculously wide, perhaps to as much as 120 degrees. You get some sense of just how wide this is when you remember that the four angles of a square are each 90 degrees. The gape of the thylacine was wider than that of a lion, which has a yawn of between 65 and 75 degrees and even *Tyrannosaurus rex*, which was able to open its jaws to as much as 80 degrees, couldn't compete with the thylacine. If you're wondering, *you* can open your mouth to 26 to 30 degrees.

Unlike a wolf or dog, the thylacine had a fairly stiff tail and its legs were quite short. Its hairy coat was dense but soft. The hair itself was about 15mm long. Its body grew to a maximum length of around 130cm from the tip of the nose to the base of the tail, and the tail added another 50-65cm to the total length. The usual weight was somewhere between 12 and 22kg, which is as much as a medium-sized dog breed such as a Bassett hound, dalmatian or springer spaniel, but the thylacine could reach a weight of up to 30kg, and usually, the males were bigger and heavier than the females.

Fifty thousand years ago, a thylacine meets a *Thylacoleo* (THY-lakko-LEO), which was one of the largest marsupial predators and among the most specialised carnivorous mammals ever.

There has been some disagreement over just how good the thylacine's sense of smell was. Early research suggested it had a very good sense of smell, which it used to sniff down prey, but recent research, using more advanced techniques, has been able to analyse the brain to see how different parts were developed for different roles. This research showed the areas dedicated to smell were not well developed in the brain, which would mean thylacine didn't use its sense of smell as much as other senses, such as its hearing and sight.

One thing that helps define not only the thylacine but also the wider marsupial group is the presence of a protective pouch in nearly all of them. In this pouch the undeveloped young can spend time in safety getting stronger and bigger and growing to the point where they're ready to face the world. As you'd expect with the group, female thylacines

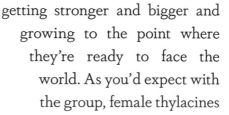

Brown-eared woolly opossum (*Caluromys lanatus*)

Koala
(*Phascolarctos cinereus*)

did indeed have a pouch. What you might *not* expect is that like the wombat, the thylacine had a backward-facing pouch. What you *really* might not expect is that it wasn't just female thylacines which had pouches but the males too.

The marsupials (mar-SOOP E-als) are a special bunch of mammals and they have a special bunch of features. For example, most marsupial species don't have bony kneecaps like most other mammals, and their skulls have extra holes in extra places, such as in the bony ring at the front of the eye socket and in the bony plate on the roof of the mouth. Apart from wombats, other marsupials have a different number of incisor (in-SI-zor) teeth at the front

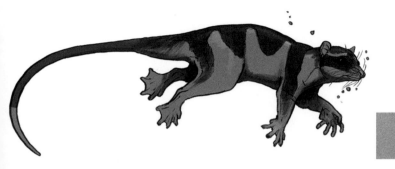

Water opossum
(*Chironectes minimus*)

Silky shrew opossum
(*Caenolestes fuliginosus*)

of the mouth when you compare their upper and lower jaws, whereas this isn't the case in most mammals, such as wolves, rats and even us. Red kangaroos, for example, have two incisor teeth on the top and six on the bottom, and the thylacine had eight incisors on the top and six on the bottom.

Another feature seen among marsupials is the pair of little bones which sit at the front of the pelvis, facing forward in the

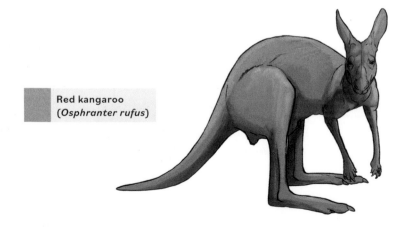

Red kangaroo
(*Osphranter rufus*)

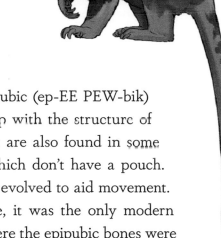

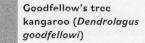
Goodfellow's tree kangaroo (*Dendrolagus goodfellowi*)

hips. These are the epipubic (ep-EE PEW-bik) bones, which might help with the structure of the mother's pouch, but are also found in some males and in species which don't have a pouch. It seems they originally evolved to aid movement. Unique to the thylacine, it was the only modern species of marsupial where the epipubic bones were made mostly from cartilage and not bone.

Northern three-striped opossum (*Monodelphis americana*)

CLASSIFICATION

When the first scientific description of the thylacine was made in 1808, it was placed into the American opossums group. And like every species that has been described in a scientific manner, the thylacine was given a two-part scientific name, also known as its binomial (BI-no ME-al) name. Ours is *Homo sapiens* (ho-mo SAY-PEE-ens), which means 'human that's wise', the blue whale is *Balaenoptera musculus* (BAY-LEEN-op-ter-a mus-CU-lus), which might be a playful twist on words which interpret as 'winged-whale mouse', and the honey bee is *Apis mellifera* (AYP-iss mell-if-er-a), which means 'bee which carries honey'. Each name is unique to that species, has two parts and is written in *italics*.

Numbat (*Myrmecobius fasciatus*)

Virginia opossum
(*Didelphis virginiana*)

The thylacine was originally given the name
Didelphis cynocephala (DI-del-fiss SY-no-seff-al-a), which means the 'dog-headed opossum'. In 1824, after realising the thylacine wasn't really that similar to the American opossums after all, it was put into its own group, *Thylacinus* (THY-la SEEN-us), which means 'sack' or 'pouch'. Even though this is the scientific name we still use, 'pouched dog-head' is a bit confusing. Confusion over the classification of the thylacine dated to much earlier than 1808, however, because as far back as the 1640s it was compared to a tiger, when European explorers first arrived on Tasmania.

When we think of mammals, we think of cats, dogs, bats, rats, badgers, whales, monkeys, moles, bears, lions, weasels and any of the several thousand mammals

Southern hairy-nosed wombat (*Lasiorhinus latifrons*)

which give birth to live young which have developed inside their mother and have been kept alive throughout pregnancy by a special organ called the placenta (plas-sen terr). This is the largest of the three groups of mammals, but there are two other groups: the monotremes (mon-O-TREEMS), which don't use a placenta but lay eggs; and the marsupials, which use a different type of placenta, have a much, much shorter pregnancy and give birth to babies which finish developing in a protective pouch on the mum.

In the monotreme group, we find the aquatic and venomous duck-billed platypus (plat-EE puss) and the spiny burrowing echidnas (EE-kid-nerz). The marsupial group is much wider and has some well-known animals including kangaroos, wallabies and koalas, wombats and Tasmanian devils, as well as some less well-known animals such as quolls, dunnarts, potoroos and the bizarre little *Antechinus* (an-TEE KIY-nuss). The thylacine also belonged to this fascinating group of pouched mammals, which are also known as metatherians (metta-theer E-ans).

There are over 330 living species of marsupials found in the wild on either the continents of Australia (about 70 per cent of them) or South America, although a few species are found in Central and North America. The marsupials appear to have split from the other mammals around 65 million years ago, not long after the asteroid killed off most of the dinosaurs at the end of the Cretaceous period.

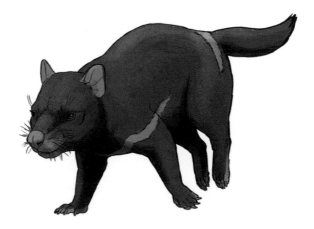

Tasmanian devil
(*Sarcophilus harrisii*)

Unlike kangaroos and wallabies, where there are quite a few different species, there was only one species of thylacine, and it was the only animal within the *Thylacinus* group. The modern thylacine probably appeared about two million years ago, during the Early Pleistocene period, but the group which would directly lead to the thylacine seems to have first appeared in the fossil record somewhere between 28 and 23 million years ago, in a period of time called the Late Oligocene (OLLY-go SEEN). A small, 10kg animal called *Badjcinus turnbulli* (badj-SEEN-us turn-bull-ii) seems to be the earliest member of the thylacine group.

There are at least 12 species in the group which contains the thylacine, a group called the Thylacinidae (THY-la-SEEN i-DAY), and the earliest members of this group ate small reptiles, small mammals and insects.

By about 20 million years ago, the fossils show the diet of thylacine ancestors had become more carnivorous. By 10 million years ago, there were several species of the thylacine, including *Thylacinus megiriani* (THY-la-SEEN-us meg-ir-EE-ARNI) and *Thylacinus potens* (THY-la-SEEN-us po-tens), which were both around the size and weight of a wolf and much larger than the most recent and well-known species of thylacine.

In terms of more well-known marsupials, the thylacine appears to have been most closely related to Tasmanian devils and other marsupial carnivores, such as dunnarts and quolls, and much more distantly to the extinct, lion-sized *Thylacoleo*, which, due its unusual teeth, may have been the most specialised predatory mammal ever.

Lots of species change their environments. Elephants maintain grasslands in Africa by eating the vegetation. If elephant populations are killed, scrubby bushes and more trees then replace the important grassland habitats.

ECOLOGY

Every single species is like a jigsaw piece in a huge, complicated puzzle. It only fits in one space and it fits in that space perfectly. A species has its unique place in a big environmental puzzle. The role a species has in its environment and the 'space' it fits into within that much larger puzzle is called its ecology. The role a species has and the relationship it has with other species and its environment varies massively, but the species and the environment are closely linked in a tight relationship. The success of one affects the future of the other.

Elephants, for example, have a huge impact on their environment and change both the plants and other animals across their habitat. If the elephant population drops or even disappears, then all the plant life in the area changes and more grows. This might sound great, but in fact, open grasslands with a few mature trees are replaced with loads of bushes and smaller trees and suddenly the animals which lived and thrived there have to move on to find habitat similar to what they're used to. Sometimes, removing one species from an ecosystem changes the whole ecology.

As humans, we like
to think we have control
over our environment but
actually, our environment
controls us too. It shapes our
evolution and explains, for example,
how whales evolved from small,
four-legged carnivorous land mammals
more than 50 million years ago, over time losing
their legs and hair, evolving fins and becoming massive, to
suit their new marine environment.

If our environments can influence and shape us, then it makes sense to think that the *same* sort of environment can produce similar adaptations and body shapes in *different* animal groups. When this happens, a very special type of evolution occurs. We call this convergent (con-ver jent) evolution and it happens when the same pressures within an environment (or a type of environment) affect the evolution of two different groups of organisms, making them evolve in a similar way.

One of the most famous examples of convergent evolution is wings in vertebrates. If you're going to fly, you need wings which allow you to fly. The ecology is the same – it's the same air, the same gravity, the same need to stay up in the air – and there are only so many ways for evolution to overcome this problem. Three very different groups have evolved methods for flying: bats have five very long fingers, which stretch the skin of the wing out; birds have wings formed from the reduced remains of bones from three finger digits; and extinct pterosaurs had three normal-sized fingers and an extremely long fourth finger, which stretched the wing from the tip of that digit to somewhere down by the legs.

Although birds, bats and pterosaurs are not closely related *at all*, these three groups show convergent evolution in their wings. It's called convergent evolution because if several things converge, they meet, so it's like evolution has made these different groups meet, or converge, on one thing. In this example, it's flight.

There are lots of examples of convergent evolution, including the thylacine and canids, or members of the dog family. Both had sharp teeth and powerful jaws, heels

Convergent evolution: wings in vertebrates

Pterosaur

Bird

Bat

As scientists, we need to follow the evidence and facts. Thylacines were rumoured to kill sheep, but research has shown they hunted much smaller prey. This thylacine is about to snack on an unlucky bandicoot.

raised off the ground and the same general body shape. Yet despite looking so similar, the thylacine and foxes, wolves and dogs haven't shared a common ancestor for over 150 million years. During this time, with members of the dog family evolving in the northern hemisphere and the thylacine evolving in the southern hemisphere, the two groups found themselves in similar habitats, feeding in some similar ways, with similar ecologies. Many people believe the thylacine and canids example is the clearest case of convergent evolution in mammals.

When we look at the actual ecology of the thylacine, it seems it was a nocturnal and crepuscular (crep-us KU-lar) predator, hunting around dawn and dusk; it would probably have hidden throughout the day in undergrowth or in dens. Although it was described as being fierce by those who wanted it hunted into extinction, the thylacine was in fact secretive and shy. Although we know the thylacine was a predator, we still don't know that much about its hunting ecology. Science often changes, as techniques improve or we have more data, so because of that our levels of understanding change too. That is one of the coolest and most interesting things about being a scientist, as it means there is always more to learn.

Some research shows that the thylacine had weak jaws and that a 30kg adult could only bite much smaller prey, weighing around 5kg. This is much less than you'd expect from a predator of that size. This would mean it was hunting small prey, like possums and bandicoots. Other research has found that the weight of a thylacine was less than 30kg, and the average was around 17kg, meaning its prey would have been even smaller. Both pieces of research disagree with an earlier finding that the thylacine may have had a powerful bite and that it was able to tackle prey as big, or even bigger, than itself. While it seems unlikely the thylacine hunted and killed sheep, and it appears it specialised in hunting much smaller animals, we won't know for sure about this important part of their ecology until we have more data and clearer results.

When

Fossil evidence shows that the species appeared about two million years ago during the Early Pleistocene (PLI-STO SEEN). Although we are not 100 per cent certain of this date just yet, we do have a specific extinction date, with the last known thylacine dying on 7 September 1936.

Where

Despite being known as the *Tasmanian* tiger, the thylacine was once found over a relatively wide area throughout the continent, across Papua New Guinea and mainland Australia, but we know from mummified remains and cave art created by people that the thylacine disappeared from the Australian mainland around 2,000 years ago. After disappearing from much of its range, the last area of safety for the thylacine was the island of Tasmania.

Environment

The Earth is pretty old. To more easily understand that vast expanse of time, incorporating the hundreds of millions, and billions, of years, we've broken it down into more manageable chunks, including longer stretches of time called eras and shorter sessions called periods. Often, these phases are based on sections of time which have similarities and might be, for example, periods when the planet was warmer or cooler or drier. But the Pleistocene, which sat within the larger Quaternary (kwa-TUR-na-ree) period, played by different rules and instead was cold, then warm, then cold, then warm, then cold again and so on and so on. You may not have heard of the Pleistocene but you'll almost definitely have heard of another name given to this phase: the 'Ice Age'. It was not long after the Pleistocene had started, around two million years ago, that the first thylacine turns up in the fossil record. For the next million and a half years or so, the world around the thylacine was constantly changing.

Overall, it was a time of intense climate instability around the world, but rather than one ice age, also known as a glacial (GLAY-SEE al) period, there were many. There were at least 20 glacials in the first phase of the Pleistocene alone, stretching over three-quarters of a million years or so. Between these glacial periods were calm phases, called interglacial (in-ter GLAY-SEE al) periods, and it was during these that biodiversity was able to flourish around the world. These interglacials would have been warm, but with extremes of rainfall, from widespread flooding to droughts. This would have created a highly stressful environment, which would have led to more species evolving around the world, everywhere from forests and jungles to grasslands and deserts.

Overall, in the northern hemisphere, vast ice sheets began to grow during glacial periods. At times, the sea level over the entire surface of the Earth would have been at least 100m lower than it is today, leaving large areas of coastal habitats dry. This water would have been locked up in huge glaciers and ice sheets, which were as much as an impressive 3km thick in some places, over much of North America and Europe. At its coldest, 30 per cent of the Earth's surface was covered by ice. The southern hemisphere was also affected and Antarctica was covered in ice, as was a large part of South America. Glaciers were also found on both New Zealand and Tasmania.

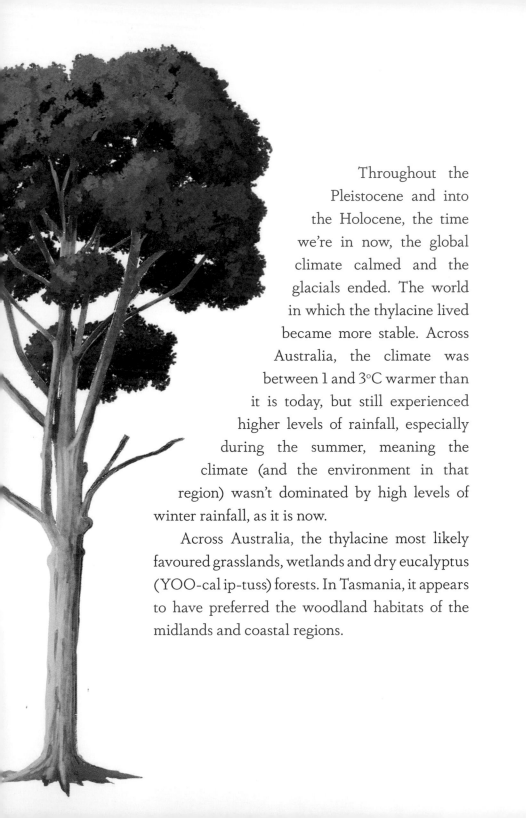

Throughout the Pleistocene and into the Holocene, the time we're in now, the global climate calmed and the glacials ended. The world in which the thylacine lived became more stable. Across Australia, the climate was between 1 and 3°C warmer than it is today, but still experienced higher levels of rainfall, especially during the summer, meaning the climate (and the environment in that region) wasn't dominated by high levels of winter rainfall, as it is now.

Across Australia, the thylacine most likely favoured grasslands, wetlands and dry eucalyptus (YOO-cal ip-tuss) forests. In Tasmania, it appears to have preferred the woodland habitats of the midlands and coastal regions.

Flora and fauna

If I ask you to picture the animals found in Australia and its neighbouring islands, I can almost guarantee you'll instantly think of kangaroos and wallabies. Maybe you've thrown a koala in as well and possibly even a Tasmanian devil, for good measure. Along with the water-loving platypus, the spiny, egg-laying echidna and a whole range of colourful birds, fascinating spiders and beautiful snakes, the animals from this particular part of the world are as fascinating, weird and wonderful as those found anywhere else on the planet. But if we include some of the animals which have now gone extinct across the continent, then it's clear the fauna from this region is not only overlooked or unappreciated, but is quite simply astounding.

The largest marsupial to have ever lived, the *Diprotodon* (DI-pro tow-don) was a supersized version of a wombat. At 2m in height, it would have been taller than an adult human and weighed around 2 tonnes, the same as an average car. These massive herbivores appear to have had a social structure similar to that seen in elephants, migrating from one area to another in huge herds. Hundreds of *Diprotodon* skeletons were found in Lake Callabonna in South Australia, after the animals appear to have become trapped in the mud around this ancient salt lake. These marsupial giants went extinct around 44,000 years ago.

Diprotodon optatum

*Procoptodon
goliah*

Whereas the
largest kangaroo
species alive today,
the red kangaroo,
reaches heights of up
to 1.8m and can weigh
as much as 85kg (about
the same height and weight
as me, near enough), the largest
species of kangaroo ever was much
bigger. The giant short-faced kangaroo
(*Procoptodon*) reached a height of up to 3m and
weighed as much as 230kg. If you think this seems
too heavy for it to bounce around like most kangaroos,
then you'd be right, as it seems these giants could not
hop. Instead, they shuffled and walked around more like

Thylacoleo carnifex

humans, before going extinct at some point 45,000–18,000 years ago.

Such large herbivores allowed the presence of equally large and impressive carnivores and there were some bizarre yet formidable predators alive throughout the Pleistocene period, alongside the thylacine. The largest of these was *Thylacoleo*. Although the name translates as 'pouched lion', it wasn't closely related to a lion at all, despite being similar in size. It is actually more accurate to say *Thylacoleo* was a carnivorous version of *Diprotodon*, but the specialised chisel-like teeth at the front of the skull and its large shearing cheek teeth may have given this

*Wonambi
naracoortensis*

hunter the greatest bite force of any mammal species ever, for its size.

It wasn't just the mammals which were large and wonderful during the Pleistocene across the Australian continent. Other groups include a snake called *Wonambi naracoortensis* (wonn-am-BEE narr-acco or-ten-sis), which grew to about 6m long and crushed its prey, or the 3m-tall *Dromornis* (drom-or niss) or Stirton's thunder bird. Weighing nearly half a tonne, about the same as a horse, this was one of the largest birds ever to have existed. Although they looked a little like ostriches or emus, these massive omnivorous birds were more closely related to ducks and geese.

Varanus priscus

Nowadays, the largest species of lizards are the Komodo dragons, but throughout the Pleistocene a true reptilian giant lived in Australia. Growing to as much as 7m in length and weighing almost 2 tonnes, a huge species of *Varanus* (va-ran-uss) goanna lizard called Megalania (mega-LAYN-EE-a) would have been a fearsome predator and the largest terrestrial lizard ever.

Palorchestes azael

Even the herbivores were scarily impressive, as demonstrated by the massive *Meiolania* (MI-O LAY-NEE-ah). This huge shelled reptile was an ancient relative of the modern turtles and tortoises alive today. Despite being among the largest members of its group, *Meiolania* specialised in eating plants along the coastline. But as with so many herbivores, *Meiolania* was not defenceless and this 2.5m-long reptile had a heavy domed shell for protection, bony horns on its head and a spiky tail for defence, similar to the tails seen in some armoured dinosaurs such as *Ankylosaurus* (an-KEE-LO sore-us).

Meiolania brevicollis

Behaviour

The thylacine was a vicious killer, chasing as many sheep as it could find, before drinking their blood in a frenzy. With a reputation like this, no wonder people either feared them or wanted them exterminated. When the decision was made to hunt them into extinction, you would have hoped that at the very least we understood their behaviour and whether they did act in a way that maybe explained why they were all killed off, right? Sadly, that was not the case and we could not have been more wrong about this quirky little carnivore.

Not only was the thylacine called the Tasmanian tiger, it was also known as the marsupial wolf, because despite having stripes like a tiger, the skull and body shape looked more similar to a wolf. And for a long time, it was assumed it behaved like wolves too. One of the key characteristics about wolves' behaviour is that they chase their prey, sometimes for hours, until it's exhausted and can finally be captured. If we look at the overall shape of the head and body of the thylacine, then yes, it's easy to see why they might have been pursuit predators but science is about looking at all the evidence and following *every* clue, so to really understand how the thylacine hunted, a thorough examination of the entire body needed to be made.

The answer to how the thylacine hunted came from a pretty unlikely source and, of all the possible parts of the skeleton it could have been, it was the elbow joint which provided the answer.

The shape of the bones around the elbow can help show us how animals move. In wolves, the end of the humerus (HYEW mer-uss), the long bone between the elbow and the shoulder, is shaped in a way that only allows the joint to open and close in what seems like a straight line. Open, close. Open, close. There's almost no side-to-side movement. This is perfect for running long distances if you want to outrun your prey and use stamina.

If the thylacine hunted in a way similar to wolves, we'd expect these bones to look the same. But the humerus shape in the thylacine was different and had some side-to-side movement, as well as the 'opening and closing' seen in the wolf.

When scientists compared this sort of bone shape with other predators, they found it was most similar to big cats such as panthers, which ambush their prey using short bursts of speed rather than long chases. Ambush predators not only leap and pounce in different directions, but also often use their front paws to grapple their prey to the ground. Based on this evidence, the scientists were about 95 per cent certain that the thylacine waited until prey got close enough for them to pounce, rather than chasing it for long distances. So although it's not really correct to call them either Tasmanian tigers or marsupial wolves, based on the way they hunted at least, 'Tasmanian tiger' seems the more accurate of the two.

It's easy to get wrapped up with the *predatory* side of the thylacine, when thinking about its behaviour, but it belongs to the fascinating group of mammals called the marsupials, and to be able to qualify for membership of that slightly strange group, it had some pretty cool behaviours. One of the key defining features of the group is having a pouch, which is hard to forget, bearing in mind we know that 'thylacine' translates from Greek via Latin as the 'dog-headed *pouched* one'.

Although a pouch is one of the most obvious features of a marsupial, it's almost an afterthought of a more important feature, which is to give birth to their young much earlier than most mammals, such as humans, dogs, cats, mice, whales, horses, rats, pangolins, elephants and even bats. We all produce our young internally over a much longer period, with the use of a protective uterus (YEW-ter-us) and a nourishing placenta.

Young marsupials are born much earlier and are not as fully formed. They are blind and hairless at this stage. This is dangerous for the tiny, defenceless baby, which still has a lot of growing to do, but it means that if there is a particularly hot, dry or wet season, there is less stress on a mother which would otherwise be supporting a developing embryo inside her body.

If conditions *are* all fine, then the bean-sized baby wriggles to the safety of the pouch, where it will spend the next few months developing. It might only have to wriggle a few centimetres to safety but that can be a massive and exhausting journey if you're tiny and haven't finished growing. To help them, marsupial babies have developed faces and strong little forelimbs with paws which are able to cling on to mum's hair, to help them make their first, perilous journey.

The time baby marsupials (known as 'joeys') spend developing inside their mothers varies from around five weeks to as little as 12 days in some species, before being born and crawling off to their pouch. It's thought that thylacine joeys spent about three months developing in the pouch, feeding on milk and learning skills they'd need to survive in the big world outside the pouch. The thylacine could have as many as four babies each time, but two or three seemed to be more common. Some marsupials breed at certain times of the year, but it seems as though the thylacine was able to breed throughout the

year, although it may have preferred the winter and spring months. We only know this because when people hunted them to collect a reward from the government, historical documents show thylacine joeys could be caught at any time of the year, rather than during one breeding season.

Caring for their young, and most likely ambushing small prey, the thylacine was not the 'big bad wolf' equivalent in the Australia region. It was a secretive and unique carnivore, integral to its ecology and not responsible for the death of countless sheep and other farm animals, as many insisted at the time. We know this, and so much more, now but if we'd stopped, looked and listened when we still had the chance, then maybe we wouldn't have needlessly blamed, hunted and killed what was surely one of the most iconic and beautiful predators the world has ever seen. Our only hope is that the sad loss of the thylacine will act as a lesson to us all to better understand the natural world, and to help us avoid future catastrophes like this.

GLOSSARY

Anatomy
An area of science which focuses on the bodily structure of animals (including humans) and other living organisms.

Apex predator
Any predator at the top of a food chain. Sometimes an apex predator will kill and eat other predators. This is also known as hyper-predation.

Biodiversity (BI-O DIE-vers it-EE)
The variety of plants, fungi, animals and other groups of organisms within a particular habitat or ecosystem. A healthy habitat or ecosystem will usually have higher levels of biodiversity.

Cartilage (car-til-aj)
The flexible yet strong substance found throughout our skeletons, most often between joints. Our nose and ears are also made from cartilage.

Crepuscular (crep-us KU-lar)
Two small windows of time each day: early in the morning, as it's getting light, and at dusk, as it's getting dark. This is my all-time favourite word.

Ecology
The particular area of biology where the focus is on the relationship between organisms and their physical surroundings.

Ecosystem
The community of organisms (animals, plants and other major groups) and their physical environment.

Epipubic (ep-EE PEW-bik) bones
These are also known as marsupial bones and are found in marsupials, in pairs at the top of the pelvis.

Eucalyptus (YOO-cal ip-tuss)
A large group of over 700 species of trees and shrubs, mostly found in Australia.

Extinct
If a species, or group of species, no longer exists, it is said to be extinct. If so few are left that they can no longer breed, even though some are alive, then the species, or group, is known as being *functionally* extinct.

Forelimbs
The front pair of limbs in an animal. These can be the arms in a human, flippers in a whale or the front pair of legs in a dog, for example.

Herbivore
An animal that has a diet based on plants.

Hybridisation
The process by which an animal, plant, etc. breeds with an individual of another species or subspecies.

Incisor (in-SI-zor)
The small, flattened teeth which sit at the front of the mouth between the canines. The incisors have a sharp cutting edge to either tear vegetation or meat.

Natural selection
The main process that brings about evolution, where organisms that are better adapted to their environment have a better chance of surviving and therefore a better chance of producing more offspring.

Omnivorous
Able to eat a combination of plants and animals.

Organism (or-gan IZ-mm)
Any living thing. A tree is an organism, so is a shark, and a mushroom. *You* are an organism.

Placenta (plas-sen terr)
An organ that develops during pregnancy and is attached to the wall of the uterus. The placenta attaches to the developing foetus via an umbilical cord. Blood from the mother passes through the placenta, filtering oxygen, nutrients and waste either to or away from the developing baby.

Terrestrial
On the land.

Uterus (YEW-ter-us)
Also known as the womb, this organ sits within the female abdomen of most mammal species. The uterus provides a secure environment for the developing foetus (or baby), in which it can be nourished, until it is born.

Collect all eight titles in the EXTINCT series

One of the oldest and most mysterious animals ever described, *Hallucigenia* was a kind of sea-living, armoured worm. But it was nothing like the worms we know today. Its body was covered in spines and frills. It had claws at the end of its legs and a mouth lined with sharp teeth.

This strange animal was one of the victims of the End Ordovician mass extinction which claimed 85 per cent of the species living in the world's oceans around 443 million years ago. What could have led to this catastrophe and what caused the appearance of huge glaciers and falling sea levels, leaving many marine ecosystems dry and unable to sustain life at a time when it had only just got started?

An armoured fish with a bite 10 times more powerful than that of a great white shark, *Dunkleosteus* could also snap its jaws five times faster than you can blink! It was one of the most iconic predators ever to rule the waves. What was it like to live in its shadow? And how did it become one of the many victims of the Late Devonian mass extinction around 375 million years ago?

Let's discover why this mass extinction only affected ocean life and why it went on for so long – some scientists believe it lasted for 25 million years. In a weird twist, we'll look at whether the evolution of trees on the land at that time was partly responsible for the loss of so many marine species, including *Dunkleosteus*.

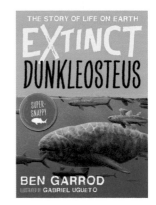

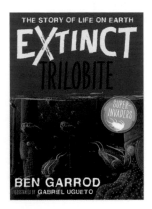

Among the first arthropods – animals with jointed legs such as insects and their relatives – trilobites were around on Earth for over 300 million years and survived the first two mass extinctions. There were once at least 20,000 species but all disappeared in the devastating End Permian mass extinction around 252 million years ago.

We'll look at why land animals were affected this time as well as those in the sea. An incredible 96 per cent of marine species went extinct and an almost equally terrible 70 per cent of life on land was wiped out in what is known as the 'Great Dying'. This was the closest we've come to losing all life on Earth and the planet was changed forever.

At a massive 9 tonnes, the elephant-sized *Lisowicia* was one of the largest animals on the planet during the Late Triassic. A kind of cross between a mammal and a reptile but not quite either, *Lisowicia* was a distant cousin of the ancient mammals – and they eventually led to our very own ancestors.

We'll discover why the End Triassic mass extinction happened, changing the global environment and making life impossible for around 75 per cent of species. And how, while this fourth mass extinction may have been devastating for most life on Earth, it gave one group of animals – dinosaurs – the chance to dominate the planet for millions of years.

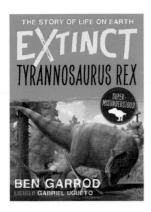

Weighing as much as three adult elephants and as long as a bus, *Tyrannosaurus rex* was one of the mightiest land predators that has ever lived. It had the most powerful bite of any dinosaur and dominated its environment. But not even the biggest dinosaurs were a match for what happened at the end of the Cretaceous, about 66 million years ago.

What happened when an asteroid travelling at almost 40,000km/h crashed into Earth? Creating a shockwave that literally shook the world, its impact threw millions of tonnes of red-hot ash and dust into the atmosphere, blocking out the sun and destroying 75 per cent of life on Earth. Any living thing bigger than a fox was gone and this fifth global mass extinction meant the end of the dinosaurs as we know them.

A giant marine predator, megalodon grew up to an incredible 18m – longer than three great white sharks, nose to tail. This ferocious monster had the most powerful bite force ever measured. It specialised in killing whales by attacking them from the side, aiming for their heart and lungs.

But, like more than 50 per cent of marine mammals and many other creatures, megalodon disappeared in the End Pliocene mass extinction around 2.5 million years ago. We'll find out why this event affected many of the bigger animals in the marine environment and had an especially bad impact on both warm-blooded animals and predators.

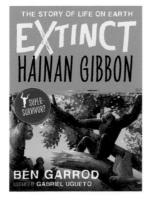

One of the most endangered animals on our planet, the Hainan gibbon is also one of our closest living relatives. Family groups of these little primates live in the trees on an island off the south coast of China and they feed on leaves and fruit.

But the gibbons are now in serious trouble because of the effects of human population increase around the world and habitat destruction. Without action, this animal might soon be extinct and need a dagger after its name. What can we all do to help stop some of our most interesting, iconic and important species from going extinct?

BEN GARROD is Professor of Evolutionary Biology and Science Engagement at the University of East Anglia. Ben has lived and worked all around the world, alongside chimpanzees in Africa, polar bears in the Arctic and giant dinosaur fossils in South America. He is currently based in the West Country. He broadcasts regularly on TV and radio and is a trustee and ambassador of a number of key conservation organisations. His eight book series *Ultimate Dinosaurs* and *The Chimpanzee and Me* are also published by Zephyr.

GABRIEL UGUETO is a scientific illustrator, palaeoartist and herpetologist based in Florida. For several years, he was an independent herpetologist researcher and authored papers on new species of neotropical lizards and various taxonomic revisions. As an illustrator, his work reflects the latest scientific hypotheses about the external appearance and the behaviour of the animals, both extinct and extant, that he reconstructs. His illustrations have appeared in books, journals, magazines, museum exhibitions and television documentaries.

Zephyr is an imprint of Head of Zeus.
At Zephyr we are proud to publish books
you can read and re-read time and time
again because they tell a brilliant story
and because they entertain you.

t @_ZephyrBooks

o @_zephyrbooks

f HeadofZeusBooks

readzephyr.com
www.headofzeus.com

ZEPHYR